EARTH

by Emma Bassier

Cody Koala
An Imprint of Pop!
popbooksonline.com

abdobooks.com

Published by Pop!, a division of ABDO, PO Box 398166, Minneapolis, Minnesota 55439. Copyright © 2021 by POP, LLC. International copyrights reserved in all countries. No part of this book may be reproduced in any form without written permission from the publisher. Pop!™ is a trademark and logo of POP, LLC.

Printed in the United States of America, North Mankato, Minnesota.

102020
012021

THIS BOOK CONTAINS RECYCLED MATERIALS

Cover Photo: Shutterstock Images
Interior Photos: Shutterstock Images, 6, 13 (top) 14, 17, 19, 20; NASA, 5 (bottom left), 5 (bottom right), 13 (bottom right); iStockphoto, 5 (top), 9; Gary Hincks/Science Source, 11; Carbon Lotus/Stocktrek Images/Science Source, 13 (bottom left)

Editor: Alyssa Krekelberg
Series Designer: Colleen McLaren

Library of Congress Control Number: 2020940299
Publisher's Cataloging-in-Publication Data
Names: Bassier, Emma, author.
Title: Earth / by Emma Bassier
Description: Minneapolis, Minnesota : POP!, 2021 | Series: Planets | Includes online resources and index
Identifiers: ISBN 9781532169076 (lib. bdg.) | ISBN 9781532169434 (ebook)
Subjects: LCSH: Earth (Planet)--Juvenile literature. | Planets--Juvenile literature. | Solar system--Juvenile literature. | Milky Way--Juvenile literature. | Space--Juvenile literature.
Classification: DDC 550--dc23

Hello! My name is

Cody Koala

Pop open this book and you'll find QR codes like this one, loaded with information, so you can learn even more!

Scan this code* and others like it while you read, or visit the website below to make this book pop.

popbooksonline.com/earth

*Scanning QR codes requires a web-enabled smart device with a QR code reader app and a camera.

Table of Contents

Chapter 1
The Third Planet 4

Chapter 2
Four Layers 8

Chapter 3
Spinning around
the Sun 12

Chapter 4
Where We Live 18

Making Connections 22
Glossary 23
Index 24
Online Resources 24

Chapter 1

The Third Planet

Earth is one of eight planets in our **solar system**. It is the third closest planet to the Sun. The Sun is a star. It is the center of the solar system.

Earth

Watch a video here!

The Sun is huge. It has powerful **gravity**. Gravity makes Earth **orbit** the Sun.

Approximately 1.3 million Earths could fit inside the Sun.

Chapter 2

Four Layers

Earth has four layers. The rocky outer layer is called the crust. Below it is the mantle. This is a thick layer of **molten rock**.

Mountains are part of Earth's crust.

Learn more here!

Metals make up Earth's core. The core has two parts. The inner core is solid. The outer core is liquid. Both are very hot.

> Temperatures in the inner core reach 9,800 degrees Fahrenheit (5,400°C).

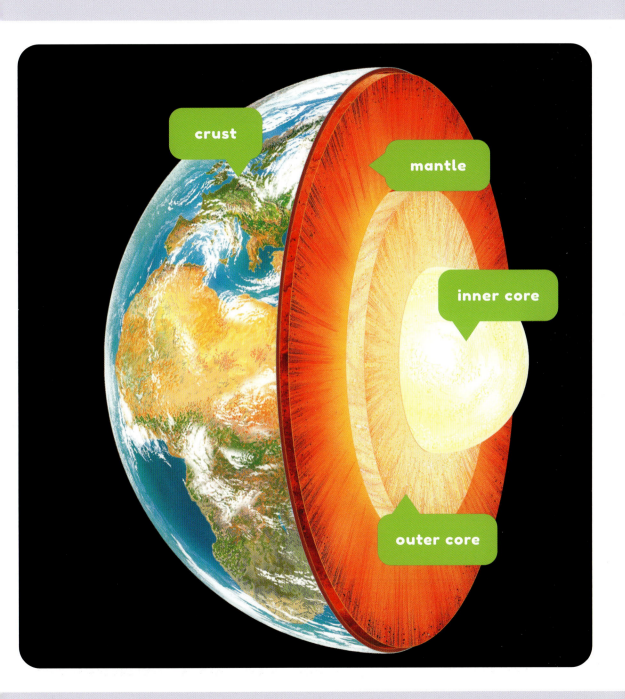

Chapter 3

Spinning around the Sun

It takes 365 days for Earth to **orbit** the Sun. Earth also spins on its **axis**. Earth makes one full spin every 24 hours. That is why one day on Earth is 24 hours long.

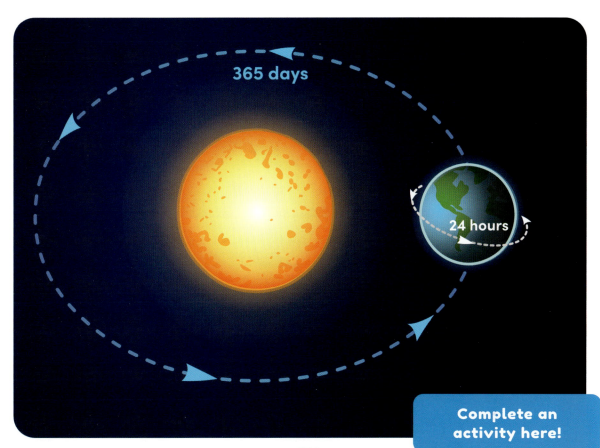

Complete an activity here!

As Earth spins, different parts of the planet face the Sun. The side facing the Sun has daytime. The other side faces away from the Sun. This side has nighttime.

Earth is tilted on its axis. The tilt of Earth as it orbits the Sun causes seasons. The part of Earth that is tipped toward the Sun is warmer. The part tipped away from the Sun is cooler.

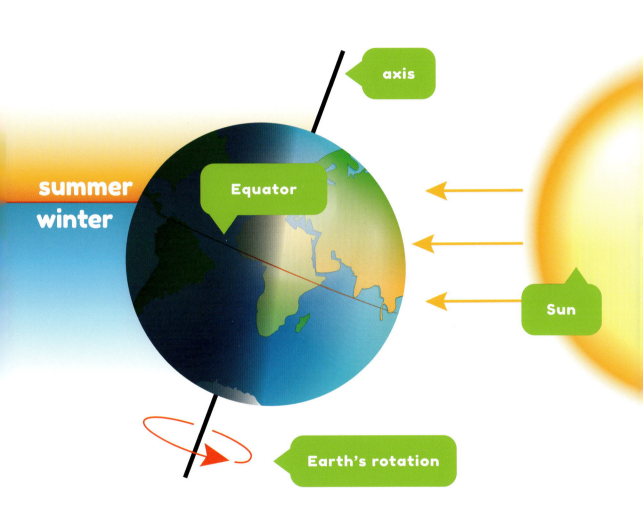

Chapter 4

Where We Live

Unlike other planets, Earth can support life. Earth is not too hot or too cold. As a result, Earth has liquid water. Living things need water to survive.

Water covers 71 percent of Earth's surface.

Earth's **atmosphere** helps support life. Living things need oxygen to breathe. The atmosphere holds oxygen. It also protects living things from the Sun. It helps keep Earth at the right temperature.

Making Connections

Text-to-Self

Most of Earth's surface is covered in water. Are there lakes, rivers, or oceans near where you live?

Text-to-Text

Have you read other books about planets? How are other planets similar to or different from Earth?

Text-to-World

Earth has seasons because its axis is tilted. What are some changes that happen on Earth during summer or winter?

Glossary

atmosphere – the layer of gas around Earth, which includes oxygen.

axis – an imaginary line that runs through the middle of a planet, from top to bottom.

gravity – a force that pulls together any objects with mass.

molten rock – hot, melted rock.

orbit – to follow a rounded path around another object.

solar system – a collection of planets and other space material orbiting a star.

Index

atmosphere, 21

axis, 12, 16, 17

gravity, 7

life, 18, 21

orbit, 7, 12, 16

seasons, 16

solar system, 4

Sun, 4, 7, 12, 15, 16, 17, 21

water, 18

Online Resources

popbooksonline.com

Thanks for reading this Cody Koala book!

Scan this code* and others like it in this book, or visit the website below to make this book pop!

popbooksonline.com/earth

*Scanning QR codes requires a web-enabled smart device with a QR code reader app and a camera.